You Know You're Middle-Aged When . . .

D0710232

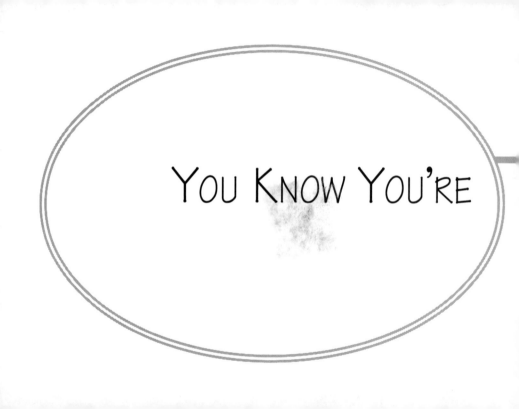

YOU KNOW YOU'RE

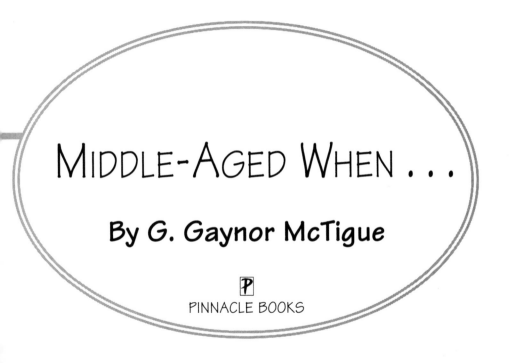

MIDDLE-AGED WHEN . . .

By G. Gaynor McTigue

P

PINNACLE BOOKS

Also by G. Gaynor McTigue

Life's Little Frustration Book

PINNACLE BOOKS are published by

Windsor Publishing Corp.
850 Third Ave
New York, NY 10022

First Pinnacle Printing: November, 1994

Printed in the United States of America

To my beautifully middle-aged wife, Beth.

INTRODUCTION

Middle age, like fog, comes on little cat feet. So subtle are its signs, you may not even know it's arrived. Or maybe you're just ignoring the symptoms, trying to squeeze the last ounce of youth out of your ripening spirit.

With this book, you can no longer hide from the truth. But why would you ever want to? The 350 telling signs of middle age contained herein will hopefully underscore how endearing, how wonderfully challenging, how downright fun middle age can be.

Read it with the understanding that, sure, you're no longer a spring chicken—but neither are you a dead duck.

Or, give this volume to a middle-aged friend or relative whom you've determined is deserving of a little roast.

Middle age. Accept it. Laugh at it. Enjoy it. You'll live a whole lot longer.

Many thanks for the incisive middle age observations of Sheree Bykofsky, Mitch Achiron, Beth McTigue, John McTigue, and Janet Rosen.

G. Gaynor McTigue

1. You're older than your dentist.

2. A cruise isn't such a bad idea after all.

3. You can no longer tell the difference between film and videotape.

4. You start reading the obituaries.

5. You bring lawn chairs to outdoor concerts.

6. The policeman could be your son.

7. Things you did as a youth now terrify you.

8. You realize your doctor is just another guy out to make a buck.

9. Life insurance suddenly makes sense.

10. Life suddenly *doesn't* make sense.

11. You no longer sit on the floor in airports, waiting rooms, and hallways.

12. You confirm your appointments.

13. You begin to think it was better in your day.

14. You wear that comfortable sweater, even though it has a hole in it.

19. You need reading glasses . . .

20. . . . then keep forgetting where you put them.

21. Instead of splitting the check, you now fight over it.

22. You realize you're never going to be "discovered."

23. Songs you used to freak out to are now Muzak.

24. You enter a store and totally forget what you came in for.

25. You try to figure out what other people are worth.

26. Finally, you get rid of your pimples.

27. You save your ties for when they come back in style.

28. Who directed it is more important than who's in it.

29. You schedule sex.

30. You call teenage boys "fellas."

31. You change from the fast lane to the scenic route.

32. You start buying those souvenirs you always wondered who bought.

33. You feel funny about walking through a restaurant with your drink.

34. You button buttons that you used to leave open.

35. Every little ache is the beginning of the end.

36. Your train of thought frequently derails.

37. Jaded expressions like "A stitch in time saves nine" and "Don't count your chickens before they hatch" suddenly seem fresh and meaningful.

38. You retire your cutoffs.

39. Old people are now elderly people.

40. You're no longer the last to leave a party.

41. In fact, you're often the first!

42. You drink beer from a glass instead of a bottle.

43. You used to seek out crowds. Now you avoid them.

44. You read the fine print . . .

45. . . . if you can see it.

46. Now, you slow down for the yellow lights.

47. It takes you two tries to get up from the couch.

48. You look at trees, rocks, and buildings and think: "They'll still be here when I'm gone."

49. You give your friends birthday cards that mock their age.

50. Your computer has more memory than you do.

51. You start giving money to charities that specialize in illnesses of the aged.

52. Rather than walk over and change the channel, you'll spend fifteen minutes looking for the remote.

53. You used to vote your conscience. Now you vote your wallet.

54. It takes you three days to recover from raking the leaves.

55. Teenagers who do the same stupid things you did . . . should know better.

56. You fill your house with junk you think you might use someday . . . but never do.

57. The time between visits with your childhood friends gets longer and longer.

58. You eye the privileges extended to senior citizens with mounting envy.

59. You need a news update at least three times a day. (Weather, six.)

60. You no longer tell anyone (except the IRS) how much you make.

61. You treat people with colds like they have the plague.

62. You change out of your clothes as soon as you get home.

63. You no longer take any crap from surly waiters.

64. You throw on a sport jacket for casual gatherings . . . just to be safe.

65. Fifty suddenly seems young.

66. Sixty suddenly seems young.

67. You don't have bad hair days. You have bad hair years.

68. You're less particular who you include in your sexual fantasies.

69. You can't ask your friends to help you move anymore.

70. You find yourself telling the same stories over . . . and over . . . and over.

71. Thank God for bigger golf clubs and larger tennis rackets!

72. It's no longer neat to stay up all night.

73. You experience irregularity with more regularity.

74. You used to walk up and down escalators. Now you settle in for the ride.

75. You eat pizza with a knife and fork.

76. Your hatred of taxes escalates.

77. You can't believe how ridiculous you looked just ten years ago.

78. You have this recurring dream that you've missed your final exams.

79. You sometimes imagine what it would have been like if you had married _____.

80. You realize your siblings are never going to treat you any differently than they did when you were kids.

81. You wear dorky things like rubbers, hats, and earmuffs.

82. Finally, you can use words like "titillate," "shuttlecock," and "Uranus" without laughing.

83. You don't sleep well anywhere but in your own bed.

84. Lawrence Welk used to make you gag. Now you watch the reruns.

85. Your parents need you more than you need them.

86. You view those with less expensive cars as common, and those with more expensive cars as showoffs.

87. When you clean out a drawer, you get hung up looking at old letters and photographs.

88. The last twenty years seem like five.

89. You no longer argue with your spouse in restaurants.

90. You can see the light at the end of your mortgage.

91. You once yearned for business travel. Now you hate it.

92. You don't renew your subscription to *Rolling Stone*.

93. You find yourself turning lights off . . . and the thermostat down.

94. A telephone rings on the TV and you think it's yours.

95. You now find polkas lusty and exhilarating.

96. You nap at will.

97. You keep buying things you already have.

98. You see gray hair not as a sign of aging, but as a symbol of wisdom.

99. Instead of going to the game, you'd rather stay home and watch it on TV.

100. You serve yourself smaller portions . . . but more of them.

101. You don't stay up for lunar eclipses.

102. You stop asking your friends how their parents are, because you're afraid of what the answer might be.

103. Enough with the salad bars. You want service.

104. You tend to drift more when you drive.

105. You're wary of empty restaurants . . . and weary of crowded ones.

106. You read reviews before you plunk down seven bucks for a movie.

107. You get an urge to grow things, like tomatoes and roses.

108. You become critical of other people's lifestyles, if only to justify yours.

109. You don't automatically opt for the cheapest-category car rental anymore.

110. You increasingly question the wisdom of having gotten that pierced ear, tattoo, or gold tooth.

111. No, you don't fake orgasms . . .
just their intensity.

112. You love it when people younger than you look
older than you.

113. Your kids can't believe how naive you are.

114. You used to seek out adventure. Now you're
content just to read about it.

115. Your handwriting becomes indecipherable. (Even to you.)

116. Somewhere along the line fashions changed . . . and you didn't.

117. For the first time, you feel funny about sneaking down to the lower boxes during a baseball game.

118. You do your Christmas shopping earlier and earlier.

119. You send out your Christmas cards later and later.

120. You receive more than a hundred mail order catalogs a year.

121. Whenever someone shakes your hand, you have an urge to wash it.

122. Sure, there are different ways of doing things. It's just that yours are better.

123. Rather than boast about your accomplishments . . . you prefer to let people just find out about them.

124. You have zero desire to befriend your food server.

125. You get away with shaving your legs once a week.

130. Getting the mail is one of the highlights of your day.

131. You listen to radio stations that describe themselves as easy, soft, and light.

132. You purchase products that contain low this, no that, and all-natural the other thing.

133. But you still succumb to juicy hamburgers dripping with melted cheese.

134. You lose track of your age.

135. You don't like to walk barefoot anymore.

136. You prefer to ride in the front of the bus and in the back of the train.

137. You talk about things like annuities and dietary fiber at cocktail parties.

138. You reserve ahead.

139. Younger members of the opposite sex don't even give you a passing glance.

140. You haven't been invited to a wedding in years.

141. When you finally are, it's someone's from the next generation.

142. Your toenails are starting to go.

143. You used to jump right out of bed. Now you think about it for a while.

144. You want to direct.

145. You're becoming a big fan of those "early bird" dinner specials.

146. You can still get down and funky. It's just that you can't get up.

147. You fall asleep at the theater.

148. Your arms aren't long enough to keep the newspaper in focus.

149. You've had it up to here with contractors, painters, and repairpersons.

150. You're too proud to order the cheapest entree on the menu.

151. And too cheap to order the costliest.

152. You can only take guests in small doses.

153. Now, you weigh the insurance risks before going skiing, roller skating, or body surfing.

154. For the first time, you have to deal with nose hair.

155. Your skirts are getting longer . . . and your heels are getting shorter.

156. You use phrases like "Back in '67 . . ."

157. You no longer do an accurate candle count on birthday cakes.

158. Rock stars you used to idolize are now pot-bellied and gray.

159. You watch golf on TV.

160. You start acting like your parents did. You start *looking* like your parents did!

161. You used to think about sex during other things. Now you think about other things during sex.

162. You lick your finger before turning a page.

163. See?

164. You've dramatically lowered your standards for selecting a mate.

165. You know just the right time to leave a party so you won't have to help clean up.

166. You don't know what today's comedians are talking about.

167. You've become quite inventive at extricating yourself from boring people at parties.

168. About the only deadline you take seriously anymore is April 15th.

169. You find yourself magnanimously making pledges to TV fund-raisers . . .

170. . . . but will haggle over the price of a trinket in a third-world country.

171. You're a sucker for sappy TV ads.

172. You give someone a fruitcake.

173. You begin a regimen of One-A-Day and Oil of Olay.

174. You've got a yen to know who your great-grandparents were.

175. You used to lie on a beach blanket under the sun. Now you sit in a chair under the umbrella.

176. You have to know where everyone stands in the political spectrum.

177. You make walrus-like sounds when you enter the water.

178. You're group-house'd out.

179. You've found that the best way to look like you know what's going on is to keep your mouth shut.

180. It's unnerving to think how many decades you've already lived in.

181. You've got antacids stashed all over the place.

182. You prefer to take the elevator, thank you.

183. Today's college kids are much younger looking than the mature, sophisticated person you were.

184. You'll pay more than ten bucks for a bottle of wine.

185. Corduroy is king.

186. Those prominent features that used to give you character now give you grief.

187. You develop affectations of sophistication, like crossing your sevens, or sniffing your wine.

188. You can't bring yourself to throw away old shoes.

189. You still think "the Twist" is in.

190. You don't like this idea of bagging your own groceries . . .

191. . . . but you'll pump your own gas to save a few bucks.

192. Even your "play" shirts are professionally laundered.

193. By the time you catch on to what's hip, it's already out of style.

194. It isn't cool to crash on someone else's floor anymore.

195. You no longer get dressed . . .
you *package* yourself.

196. Your idea of a vacation is to plunk yourself
down in one place and not budge for a week.

197. You'll believe it when you see it.

198. You hate New Year's Eve.

199. You deal with stressful situations in a
more mature way—you go shopping.

200. You don't dare tell your kids
what you did at their age.

201. It takes you two minutes, tops, to size a
person up.

202. The Hollywood sex symbols of your youth are
now playing grandparents and retirees.

203. You can no longer get away with Melmac
and jelly glasses for dinnerware.

204. You're becoming a prune freak.

205. Your high school yearbook is good for a few belly laughs.

206. You rely on that old standby, weather, to fill in gaps in conversation.

207. You return more gifts than you keep.

208. You stay after the movie to watch the credits (even though you haven't a clue who anybody is).

209. Your mouth is an engineering marvel of root canals, bridges, and fillings.

210. Ninety percent of your dreams are reruns.

211. You used to think bunions, calluses, and corns only happened to other people.

212. If you don't write it down, you don't remember it.

213. College-age kids call you "sir" or "ma'am."

214. You eat less of the foods that require work—like pistachio nuts, watermelon, and navel oranges.

215. If you never see another marching band, it's all the same to you.

216. You find it appalling that people now talk out loud in libraries.

217. Yesterday you heard about this great idea. Today you think it was yours.

218. You realize the only way your marriage will be judged a statistical success is if you die before you get a divorce.

219. As soon as the play begins, you start wondering when it's going to be over.

220. You tell those youngsters to turn it down.

221. You're embarrassed to order a bologna sandwich in public.

222. You've learned to justify just about anything you do.

223. You finally break down and give the mail carrier something for Christmas.

224. You tell someone how great they look, and they don't return the compliment.

225. Somewhere in your sock drawer there's a pair of argyles.

226. You stay out past midnight and think you're reckless.

227. You take up a sport that will carry you through retirement.

228. You realize how many people in power and authority are just winging it.

229. Certain household projects have been staring you in the face for years . . . and will continue to stare you in the face for many years to come.

230. You open the mailbox a second time, just to make sure it went down.

231. Those cordials in your liquor cabinet must be at least ten years old.

232. You think political commercials should be banned . . . for their stupidity alone.

233. Instead of holes in your jeans, you now have creases.

234. You can't remember your phone number.

235. You begin to make self-deprecating jokes about your age.

236. When you see a dime on the ground, you don't bother to pick it up.

237. A quarter, maybe.

238. By now, your worst mistakes are behind you.

239. And your best meals are in front of you. Literally.

240. You first slept with your spouse entwined. Then it was face-to-face. Now it's back-to-back.

241. It's amazing how fast clothes shrink these days.

242. You've developed a remarkable skill for turning down people seeking donations.

243. When you watch an auto race, you no longer hope the cars will crash.

244. You never know what to get anyone anymore.

245. Your hair takes less time to dry.

246. Younger, wealthier people can't possibly be happy.

247. You leave during the third quarter, the seventh inning, or the fourth set.

248. By now, you've been ripped off
by auto mechanics to the tune of a new car.

249. And by vending machines, the equivalent of
dinner for two at Lutèce.

250. You spend the majority of your evenings
wearing out the couch.

251. You don't let it get to you.

252. If you eat another piece of cream-filled birthday cake, you'll explode.

253. The dreams you never achieved have taken on new life in your kids.

254. You're embarrassed by the appearance of your luggage as it comes around the baggage carousel.

255. You watch tabloid TV shows just to convince yourself how reprehensible they are.

256. You're self-righteously
intolerant of anyone with vices you've given up.

257. You're stuck in traffic and you think, *So what?*

258. You've been Marilyn Monroe'd, JFK'd, and
Elvis'd to death.

259. The most exciting sex you have these
days is in your dreams.

260. Never mind "high road" and "low road," you take the path of least resistance.

261. You're a little less discreet about where you choose to pass gas.

262. What we need from today's youth is a little less rebelliousness and a little more respect!

263. You take sides with one neighbor to gossip about another neighbor.

264. The only "Stones" you're interested in these days are Kidney and Gall.

265. You feel compelled to make small talk with storekeepers.

266. You meet inside the restaurant instead of outside the restaurant.

267. What a nifty idea, these cardigans!

268. Your boobs are starting to migrate south.

269. People warn you about shoveling snow.

270. You begin questioning the wisdom of working your whole life to leave your money to someone else.

271. That "Who" poster no longer seems appropriate on your living room wall.

272. You stand in front of store windows to watch tickertapes.

273. It annoys you when people drop in on you unexpectedly (even though you told them to).

274. You don't wear tie shoes around the house.

275. You've seen them come. And you've seen them go.

276. You make new friends less through shared interests than shared dislikes.

277. Financial services firms are all over you.

278. You can remember when hockey goalies didn't wear masks . . . small children traveled loose in the backs of station wagons . . . and newspapers separated the Help Wanted column into "male" and "female."

279. You subscribe to magazines that will look good on your coffee table.

280. Words like "Urgent!" and "Important!" on envelopes don't even pique your interest anymore.

281. Words like "Amazing longevity breakthrough!" do.

282. Spandex and Lycra are becoming your fabrics of choice.

283. You stop wearing old school jerseys that display the year you graduated.

284. You no longer ask people who address you as "Mr." or "Mrs." to call you by your first name.

285. Charities are starting to send you letters requesting that you include them in your will.

286. You snicker at people on TV who have morning sex before brushing their teeth.

287. You avoid delis where they make sandwiches with their bare hands.

288. When the game goes into extra innings, you go to bed.

289. You've learned that you can't trust anyone, least of all yourself.

290. You get it in writing.

291. You receive a gift subscription to Modern Maturity (and it's not a joke).

292. You fantasize taking several years off, playing nothing but golf, and qualifying for the PGA Seniors Tour.

293. By now you've had all Heinz 57 varieties.

294. You realize you're never going to catch up.

295. You have a piece of advice for everyone.

296. Your "new" overcoat is suddenly ten years old.

297. You get dizzy on footstools.

298. You've been meaning to replace that rickety ironing board for God knows how long.

299. You realize that Yogi Berra was right.

300. And Maharishi Mahesh Yogi was wrong.

301. There's one chair in the house that's your chair.

302. You're always finding forgotten cash, receipts, and gum in your coat pockets.

303. You still want your wife to look sexy, but not *that* sexy.

304. You could care less anymore if people like you.

305. It's no longer fun driving in snow.

306. You tell someone the same story they told you.

307. You eat your desserts with delicacy, grace, and small bites. But you still eat them.

308. You no longer would kill to be a professional football player.

309. You don't overload your plate at the start of the buffet line, because you know all the good stuff is at the end.

310. You fancy yourself a survivor.

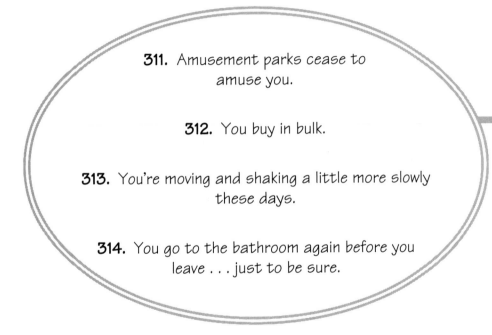

311. Amusement parks cease to amuse you.

312. You buy in bulk.

313. You're moving and shaking a little more slowly these days.

314. You go to the bathroom again before you leave . . . just to be sure.

315. You're less inclined to make
waves, ruffle feathers, or rock the boat.

316. You're a drugstore sedan-driving man.

317. You have no patience for busy signals.

318. Each day you count your blessings.
And your assets.

319. You don't discuss your personal life with anyone (except people on airplanes).

320. You finally heed the words to the song "Don't cross in the middle of the block!"

321. These days, your idea of doing the town is lunch and a matinee.

322. You can't remember if something was a dream, or actually happened.

323. You make your bathroom lighting less harsh.

324. It can wait till later.

325. You would love to read the bottom of your host's dinner plate.

326. You collect refrigerator magnets.

327. Your kids left and stuck you with the pet.

328. Somewhere in the house there's a container of quarters, dimes, and nickels.

329. Everything bad that happens in the world just goes to prove your theory.

330. You direct traffic on alternate-feed waiting lines.

331. You yearn for the days when there were just three kinds of toothpaste, 13 TV channels, and one cough remedy.

332. You point out to your kids how important it is to take care of one's parents.

333. When commercials tell you to "Be there!," you make a special point not to.

334. You're stuck in a musical time warp.

335. You no longer say no to the lobster bib.

336. You can watch a movie you've already seen and not even know it.

337. You realize that all the amazing timesaving devices you use everyday leave you with little time for yourself.

338. You never run out of gas.

339. You frequently run out of energy.

340. You hire an accordian player for your family reunion.

341. You don't like to be seen in fast-food restaurants.

342. You act seasoned and composed during airplane takeoffs, when you're just as scared as everyone else.

343. You've grown into Victor Borge's comedy.

344. You've grown out of Jerry Lewis's.

345. You realize that this is it . . . this is as good or as bad as it's ever going to get.

346. Nah!

347. Your bookshelf contains at least three of the following titles:

> *What Color Is Your Parachute?*
> *The Joy of Sex*
> *Let's Eat Right to Keep Fit*
> *The Complete Book of Running*
> *Love Story*

348. You gain what you'd like to lose, and you lose what you'd like to gain.

349. You no longer want cheap. You want nice.

350. You think about all the cockamamie things you did in your youth and you thank your lucky stars you've made it this far.